WITHDRAWN

Fact Finders®

SERIOUSLY TRUE MYSTERIES

THE CASE OF THE

Ad That Subtracts

and Other True Math Mysteries for You to Solve

by Danielle S. Hammelef

Consultant: Thomasenia Lott Adams
Professor, School of Teaching and Learning
University of Florida

CAPSTONE PRESS
a capstone imprint

Fact Finders are published by Capstone Press,
1710 Roe Crest Drive, North Mankato, Minnesota 56003.
www.capstonepub.com

Books published by Capstone Press are manufactured with paper
containing at least 10 percent post-consumer waste.

Library of Congress Cataloging-in-Publication Data
Hammelef, Danielle S.
The case of the ad that subtracts and other true math mysteries for you to solve / by Danielle S. Hammelef.
   p. cm.—(Fact finders. seriously true mysteries)
Includes bibliographical references and index.
Summary: "Nonfiction math concepts are presented as mysteries for readers to solve. With the turn of a page, readers
learn how to solve the true math mystery"—Provided by publisher.
ISBN 978-1-4296-7624-3 (library binding)
1. Word problems (Mathematics)—Juvenile literature. I. Title. II. Series.
QA63.H27 2012
510.76—dc23
                                                      2011020703

Editorial Credits
Jennifer Besel, editor; Tracy Davies McCabe, designer; Wanda Winch, media researcher;
   Laura Manthe, production specialist

Photo Credits
Capstone Studio: Karon Dubke, 19 (gecko, aquarium); Dreamstime: Martine Oger, 5 (map), Ranier, 17 (back), 18 (back);
iStockphoto Inc: Brandon Laufenberg, 25 (map), DNY59, 9 (newspaper); Shutterstock: alejandro dans neergaard, 9
(middle), Amit Erdem, 23 (back), 24 (back), Andrejs Zavadskis, 28 (back), ARENA Creative, 7 (back), 8 (back), Artistic
Endeavor, 15 (clipboard), 16 (clipboard), atoss, cover (banana), Barry Blackburn, 17 (rain gauge), bonchan, 9 (chocolate
chips), 10 (chocolate chips), cellistka, 20 (left), Christopher Hall, 11 (middle fence), clearviewstock, 11 (bottom fence),
12 (fence), Danylchenko Laroslav, cover (alarm clock), Dewitt, 24 (middle), dibrova, 4 (top), 29 (top), donatas1205, 13
(back), Fer Gregory, 15 (back diamonds), 16 (back diamonds), file404, 21 (back), 22 (back), fotomak, 25 (back), 26 (back),
hamurishi, 21 (gray, blue bikes), jannoon028, 17 (notebook), 18 (notebook), Johannes Kornelius, 20 (bottom), Karen
Roach, 6 (ruler), Kayros Studio "Be Happy!", cover (bike), 25 (computer), Kristof Degreef, cover (gecko), Liveshot, 19 (back),
20 (back), M. Unal Ozmen, 9 (back), 10 (back), Mana Photo, 5 (back), 6 (back), Mazzzur, 11 (back), 12 (back), mellerium
arkay, 15 (badge design), Morgan Lane Photography, cover (money bag), mrHanson, cover (lawn sprinkler), Neo Edmund,
27 (index card), Olga Tropinina, 21 (bubble), pashabo, cover (grid paper), 24 (coffee ring), Paul Maguire, cover (cookies),
photoroller, 23 (paper), Picsfive, 23 (cup), prism68, 13 (corkboard), 14 (corkboard), Richard Peterson, 11 (puppy), Rob
Byron, 13 (sticky note), 14 (sticky note), Rozaliya, 15 (diamond bottom left), RT Design Studio, 21 (red bike), Skyline, 4
(calculator), 29 (calculator), Sonya Etchison, cover (skateboard), Talvi, 17 (raindrop), 18 (raindrop), Tatuasha, 21 (green
bike), 22 (green bike), teena137, 15 (gold jewelry), 16 (gold jewelry), UlkaStudio, 27 (bananas), vinz89, 7 (brochure), 8
(brochure), YanLev, 28 (back), Yuri Samosonov, 13 (red tack), 14 (red tack)

Printed in the United States of America in Brainerd, Minnesota.
102011   006406BANGS12

TABLE OF CONTENTS

ON THE ANSWER TRAIL

When will the storm hit? Where is the missing money? From storm tracking to stolen loot, math mysteries are lurking everywhere. But forget the magnifying glass. You'll need some paper, a pencil, and maybe a calculator to sleuth out the answers in this book.

BEFORE CONTINUING, PLEASE STATE THE MATH DETECTIVE'S PROMISE:

I will read each one-page mystery completely. I will try to solve each mystery to the best of my ability. I will not use this book as scratch paper. I will not peek at the answer on the flip side of the page. Only after I have solved the mystery or worn down my pencil trying, may I turn the page.

That about sums it up. You are now ready to solve some math mysteries. But proceed with caution. You may experience a loss of digits.

TSUNAMI!

BULLETIN

FROM THE PACIFIC OCEAN TSUNAMI WARNING CENTER,
A TSUNAMI WARNING IS NOW IN EFFECT FOR TAHITI.

AN EARTHQUAKE LOCATED NEAR SANTIAGO, CHILE,
OCCURRED AT 6:34 AM. SEA LEVEL READINGS CONFIRM
THE EARTHQUAKE CREATED A TSUNAMI. THE TSUNAMI
IS TRAVELING WEST AT 500 MILES PER HOUR.

PACIFIC OCEAN

Tahiti

Santiago,
Chile

1 inch = 2,000 miles

HOW LONG WILL IT TAKE THE TSUNAMI TO REACH TAHITI?

TIMING THE WAVES

Every second counts when tsunamis approach. To find out how long before the waves hit Tahiti, first use the map. Take a ruler and measure how far it is from the center of the earthquake zone to Tahiti. It's about **2½ inches**. The key on the map shows that 1 inch equals **2,000 miles**. So we multiply the number of inches by the number of miles to find the actual distance between the earthquake and the island.

`2½ inches x 2,000 miles = about 5,000 miles`

Next use the information in the weather report. The report said the tsunami was traveling at a speed of 500 miles per hour. Traveling at that speed, how long will it take the tsunami to go 5,000 miles? To find out, divide the distance by the speed.

`5,000 miles ÷ 500 miles per hour = 10 hours`

It will take 10 hours for the tsunami to reach Tahiti.

CATCHING SOME AIR

Holly	Brad	Dan	Marissa
90	50	95	97
20	90	9	7
70	75	25	35
11	10	60	74
42	10	74	53

Welcome to the 5th Annual Skateboarding Spectacular!

Rules for this year's event are as follows:
- Each skater has two minutes on the course.
- The event's five judges will award points for spins, flips, airs, and grinds.
- Each skater's highest and lowest scores will be tossed out.
- The highest average score wins.

WHO IS THE WINNER OF THE SKATEBOARDING SPECTACULAR?

JUST AVERAGE

Who is the most spectacular skater? To find out, follow the rules of the event. First cross out each skater's highest and lowest scores. The scoreboard now looks like this:

Holly	Brad	Dan	Marissa
~~90~~	50	~~95~~	~~97~~
20	~~90~~	~~9~~	~~7~~
70	75	25	35
~~11~~	~~10~~	60	74
42	10	74	53

The rules stated that the highest **average** score wins. To find a skater's average score, first add his or her remaining three scores.

Holly: 20 + 70 + 42 = 132   Dan: 25 + 60 + 74 = 159
Brad: 50 + 75 + 10 = 135   Marissa: 35 + 74 + 53 = 162

Next find each skater's average. Divide each sum by the number of scores that were added together. Each skater had three remaining scores. So divide each sum by three.

Holly: 132 ÷ 3 = 44   Dan: 159 ÷ 3 = 53
Brad: 135 ÷ 3 = 45   Marissa: 162 ÷ 3 = 54

MARISSA HAS THE HIGHEST AVERAGE, SO SHE WINS.

average: a number that represents the middle of a group of numbers

SHAPING UP TO WIN

Newsy Times

BAKERIES DISAGREE WITH CONTEST RULING

Three bakeries baked giant cookies in hopes of winning the World's Largest Cookie Contest. The rules stated that the award should go to the cookie with the largest area. Judges said Rolling Pin Bakery won.

Bakeries disagree over which cookie is the largest.

Rolling Pin Bakery made a 75-foot by 50-foot rectangular cookie. The Cookie Jar Bakery argues that their 60-foot square cookie should have won. The Baker's Dozen Bakery, which baked a 70-foot diameter round cookie, also claimed the judges were wrong.

DID THE ROLLING PIN BAKERY DESERVE THE TROPHY FOR WORLD'S LARGEST COOKIE?

A LITTLE AREA

The cookie with the largest **area** should have won. Using the cookies' measurements, calculate the area of each cookie. An area of a rectangle or square is found by multiplying the length times the width. The article said the rectangular cookie was 75 feet by 50 feet.

`75 feet x 50 feet = 3,750 square feet`

The Cookie Jar Bakery's cookie was a square 60 feet long by 60 feet wide.

`60 feet x 60 feet = 3,600 square feet`

To find the area of the circular cookie, you have to understand a bit about pi. Pi is a number that helps us find the area of a circle. Pi is about 3.14. Formulas use the symbol **π** to stand for the number pi.

You can use pi and the circle's **diameter** to calculate area. The cookie's diameter was 70 feet. `π x (70 feet ÷ 2) x (70 feet ÷ 2)`
First do the math inside the parenthesis. `70 feet ÷ 2 = 35`

Then fill the answer into the formula.

`π x 35 x 35 = 3,846.5 square feet`

Now compare the cookies' areas.
`rectangular cookie — 3,750 square feet`
`square cookie — 3,600 square feet`
`circular cookie — 3,846.5 square feet`

```
Area Formulas

area of a rectangle
  length x width

area of a square
  length x width

area of a circle
  π x (diameter ÷ 2) x (diameter ÷ 2)
```

The circular cookie had the largest area. The trophy should have gone to Baker's Dozen Bakery.

area: the amount of surface in a given boundary
diameter: the length of a line segment that runs from one side to another in a circle through the center

Puppy Love

Emma and Ben's parents finally said they could get a puppy. But there's a catch. In order to get the dog, Emma and Ben have to help pay for a fence around the yard. They must pay for half of the cost to put in a fence. They have $300.

back of our House

yard

40 feet

100 feet

AFFORDABLE FENCING CO.

Chain Link Fencing:

Just $3 per foot installed

Do they have enough money?

Fenced In

The diagram of the house and yard is the key to finding out how much fencing is needed. The two sides are each 40 feet long. The back is 100 feet long. The house actually covers the fourth side, so no fencing is needed there.

To find the length of fence needed, add the lengths of the sides.
`40 feet + 40 feet + 100 feet = 180 feet`

Then use the fence ad to calculate the cost to install 180 feet of fencing. The ad says it costs $3 per foot of fencing. Multiply the total length by the cost per foot of fencing.
`180 feet x $3.00 per foot = $540.00`

Emma and Ben must only pay half of the total cost.
`$540 ÷ 2 = $270.00`

Now subtract the amount they need from the amount they have.
`$300 - $270 = $30 extra`

Yes! They have enough money for fencing. They can get their puppy, and even have some money left for dog treats.

Take Your Best Shot

Hospitals were full of people sick with the flu. Health officials advised people of all ages to get flu shots. The town organized a flu shot clinic.

Nurses brought 100 boxes of flu vaccine on the day of the clinic. Each box contained 10 adult dosages. Children ages 3 and under needed one-half the adult dosage. Children ages 4 to 10 years needed three-quarters of the adult dosage. Anyone over age 10 needed the full adult dosage.

Nurses counted up the people on the sign-in sheet. **Did they bring enough flu vaccine for everyone?**

Free flu vaccines

Wednesday

Emerson
Elementary
School Gym

3 p.m. to 9 p.m.

People over age 10	People ages 4 to 10	People under age 3
500	400	300

Just the Right Dose

To find out if they brought enough medicine, you first have to figure out how many doses are needed.

Start with the kids age 3 and under. There were 300 children in this age range. Each child needed one-half of an adult dosage. To calculate the amount of dosages needed, multiply **300 x $\frac{1}{2}$**. To multiply a whole number by a fraction, first change the whole number into a fraction. Any whole number can be written as $\frac{itself}{1}$. The number 300 becomes the fraction $\frac{300}{1}$. Multiply the top two numbers, called the numerators. Then multiply the bottom numbers, called denominators. $\frac{300}{1}$ **x** $\frac{1}{2}$ **=** $\frac{300}{2}$

Next divide the top number by the bottom.
300 ÷ 2 = 150 adult dosages

Complete a similar calculation for the 4- to 10-year-olds. They needed three-quarters, or $\frac{3}{4}$, of an adult dosage. $\frac{400}{1}$ **x** $\frac{3}{4}$ **=** $\frac{1200}{4}$

1,200 ÷ 4 = 300 adult dosages

Five hundred people over age 10 needed shots. Each of these people needed a full dosage. Add the dosages from all age groups to find the total needed.
150 + 300 + 500 = 950 adult dosages

Did the nurses bring enough vaccine? Each box contained 10 dosages. The nurses brought 100 boxes.

100 x 10 = 1,000 dosages
1,000 dosages - 950 dosages needed = 50 extra dosages

Yes, the nurses brought enough vaccine for all.

Where's the Loot?

Case Number: JT03

Incident: Jewelry theft

Reporting officer: Officer Rob

At 2:27 a.m., officers arrested Mr. Gil Tee at the west intersection of Scenic Route Drive, Main Street, and Elm Tree Road. Mr. Tee matches the picture of the robbery suspect seen on the jewelry store security camera. The camera showed Mr. Tee exiting the store at 2:15 a.m. carrying a large bag. Officers searched Mr. Tee's car but did not find the bag. I suspect Mr. Tee dumped the bag along one of the routes drawn on the map. Twelve minutes passed from 2:15 a.m. until 2:27 a.m.

Given the speed limits, which route would be traveled in 12 minutes?

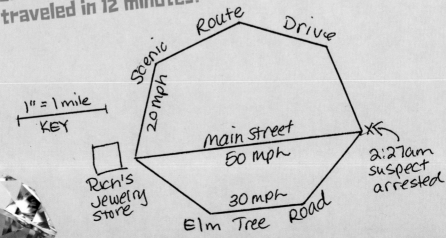

Scenic Route Drive

20mph

1" = 1 mile
KEY

Main Street
50 mph

Rich's Jewelry Store

30 mph
Elm Tree Road

2:27am suspect arrested

Treasure Hunt

The map is the key to solving this mystery. First use a ruler to measure the distance from the store to the place of arrest along each street. On Main Street, it's 2.5 inches from the store to the arrest scene. The scale says 1 inch equals 1 mile. So the route is 2.5 miles.

Do the same calculations for the other roads. The Elm Tree Road route is 3 miles. The Scenic Route Drive path is 4 miles.

The map also shows the speed limits for each road. To calculate the time it takes to travel Main Street, divide the distance by the speed limit.

`2.5 miles ÷ 50 miles per hour = 0.05 hours`

There are 60 minutes in an hour. To change hours to minutes, multiply the number of hours by 60 minutes per hour.

`0.05 hours x 60 minutes per hour = 3 minutes` to travel Main Street

Make similar calculations for Elm Tree Road. The speed limit on Elm is 30 mph. The time to travel Elm Tree Road is:

`3 miles ÷ 30 mph = 0.1 hours`
`0.1 hours x 60 minutes per hour = 6 minutes` to travel Elm Tree Road

The speed limit for Scenic Route Drive is 20 mph.

`4 miles ÷ 20 mph = 0.2 hours`
`0.2 hours x 60 minutes per hour = 12 minutes`

It takes 12 minutes to travel Scenic Route Drive. Officers will search that road for the loot.

WANT SPRINKLES ON YOUR SUNDAY?

Memo No. _____
Date   /   /

Day	Rainfall in inches
Sunday	0.14
Monday	0.08
Tuesday	0.17
Wednesday	0.00
Thursday	0.03
Friday	0.11
Saturday	0.42

Vegetable gardens need 2 inches of rain each week to grow healthy plants. The sprinkler can apply water at a rate of 0.75 inches per hour.

How many minutes should the sprinkler run to give the garden enough water for the week?

Garden Greens

Memo No. _____
Date   /   /

To find out if the garden needs more water, first check the chart. Add the daily rainfall amounts.

0.14 + 0.08 + 0.17 + 0.00 + 0.03 + 0.11 + 0.42 =

0.95 inches of rain for the week

The mystery said a healthy garden needs 2 inches of rain per week. Subtract the total rainfall the garden got from the 2 inches.

2.00 inches - 0.95 inches = 1.05 inches

The garden needs 1.05 more inches of water.

Now find out how long to run the sprinkler. Divide the water shortage by the rate water comes out of the sprinkler.

1.05 inches ÷ 0.75 inches per hour = 1.4 hours

Change the hours to minutes like you did in the missing loot mystery.

1.4 hours x 60 minutes per hour = 84 minutes

Run the sprinkler for 84 minutes, and get ready to watch your garden grow!

Tanks a Lot!

My pet gecko needs a new tank. The new aquarium has to fit on the tank stand. The stand is 24 inches long by 14 inches wide.

The pet store sells three sizes of aquariums.

Aquarium A:
12 inches long, 12 inches wide, 20 inches deep

Aquarium B:
20 inches long, 12 inches wide, 16 inches deep

Aquarium C:
20 inches long, 16 inches wide, 12 inches deep

MR. STICKY FEET

Which tank will give Mr. Sticky Feet the most room to climb and still fit on the stand?

19

Turn up the Volume

To find the tank with the most space, calculate the **volume** of each tank. Multiply the length, width, and height of each tank to get the volume in cubic inches.

Aquarium A:
12 inches x 12 inches x 20 inches = 2,880 cubic inches

Aquarium B:
20 inches x 12 inches x 16 inches = 3,840 cubic inches

Aquarium C:
20 inches x 16 inches x 12 inches = 3,840 cubic inches

Aquariums B and C have equally greater volumes than aquarium A. Now consider which tank will fit on the stand. Aquarium C is 16 inches wide. That's 2 inches wider than the stand.

The owner should buy aquarium B.
Happy climbing, Mr. Sticky Feet!

volume: the amount of space taken up by an object

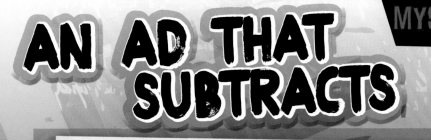

AN AD THAT SUBTRACTS

MYSTERY 9

Semiannual Sale
This Week Only!

Super Charge MX
regularly priced $120

Extreme Machine
regularly priced $150

Dynamite 6000
regularly priced $105

Gold Rush Crush
regularly priced $95

All Bikes $150 and up are 20% off!
All Bikes $100 to $149 are $20 off!
We'll pay your sales tax too!

I have $90.
Can I get a
new bike?

21

TAKING OFF

Can you buy any of the bikes with just $90? To find out, calculate the sale prices. The ad says any bike that costs $150 or more is 20 percent off. The Extreme Machine regularly costs $150. Its sale price is 20 percent less. Twenty percent is the same as 0.20. To find the sale price, first multiply the regular price by 0.20. This gives you the amount of money the sale subtracts from the original price.

$150 x 0.20 = $30

Subtract the discount from the regular price to find the Extreme Machine's sale price. **$150 - $30 = $120**

Bikes that cost between $100 and $149 are $20 off. What's the sale price of the Dynamite 6000? **$105 - $20 = $85**

Here the math for the Super Charge MX's new price.
$120 - $20 = $100

The Gold Rush Crush is not on sale. Its price stays $95.

You can buy the Dynamite 6000 for $85 and still have some money left over.

Secret Drop

From: Agent 101

To: Agent 411

We have clues to the time of a secret drop. We know it will be Tuesday at the corner of Elm and Maple. Please decode the time ASAP.

1) Number of sides of an octagon times the number of even numbers from 1 to 10

2) Area of a 4 foot by 4 foot square, doubled

3) Number of sides of five triangles minus twice the number of sets of parallel lines in a rectangle

4) Find the sum of clues 1, 2, and 3. Multiply by 100. Subtract 6,000

WHAT TIME IS THE SECRET DROP?

Crack the Code

The clues are decoded like this:

Clue 1: An octagon has eight sides. There are five even numbers from one to 10. Multiply these answers. `8 x 5 = 40`

Clue 2: The area of a square is the length times the width.
`4 feet x 4 feet = 16 feet`
Then double the answer. `16 x 2 = 32`

Clue 3: A triangle has three sides.
`3 sides x 5 triangles = 15 sides`
A rectangle has two sets of parallel lines. Twice that number is four.
Then subtract the answers. `15 - 4 = 11`

Clue 4: Add the answers to clues 1 through 3.
`40 + 32 + 11 = 83`
Then multiply the answer by 100. `83 x 100 = 8,300`
Then subtract 6,000. `8,300 - 6,000 = 2,300`

2,300 would be 2300 hours or the 23rd hour of the day.

The drop time is 11 p.m.

Time Warp

To: olivia@truemathmysteries.com
Cc:

Subject: Spring Break

Hey, Olivia! My parents and I are leaving Detroit on Friday at 6 a.m. Mom says it takes five hours to drive to your house. See you at 11 a.m. Friday!
Maria

Is Maria correct about her arrival time?

Zoning Out

Understanding time when traveling can be tricky. Look at the map above the computer screen. See how the country is divided and the clocks have different times? Those pieces of information will help unlock this mystery.

The world is divided into 24 **time zones**. Each zone is one hour earlier than the time directly to the east of it. Detroit is located in what is called the Eastern Time Zone. Chicago is in the Central Time Zone. While heading west, Maria would gain an hour when she crossed time zones. That means she would have to set her watch back an hour. The trip from Detroit to Chicago still takes five hours. But her arrival time needs to be adjusted as she crosses the time zone.

 Maria was incorrect about her arrival time. She will arrive at Olivia's at 10 a.m., not 11 a.m.

time zone: a region where the same time is used

LOW FUEL

Nutrition Facts

Serving Size 1 large banana

Amount Per Serving

Calories 125

Formula for how many calories are burned per hour of biking:

3.86 x weight in pounds x hours spent biking

Four friends are planning a one and a half hour biking trip. They need to have snacks ready for when they return. They decide to get bananas. They want to buy enough bananas to replace the calories they burn by biking.

The friends did some research. They found a formula to help them figure out how many calories biking burns. And they made a chart of all their weights.

HOW MANY BANANAS SHOULD THEY BUY?

	Weight in pounds
Christina	92
Miguel	84
Sara	108
Xavier	117

FORMULATING A PLAN

People burn calories at different rates based on how much they weigh. In the formula the magic number is **3.86**. This number is the amount of calories that a person burns per pound each hour of biking.

Plug Christina's information into the formula to find out how many calories she'll burn on the bike ride.

```
3.86 x 92 pounds x 1.5 hours = 532.68 calories
```

Round the calories to the nearest whole number, which is **533**.

Do similar calculations for the other kids, and you end up with these numbers.

	Weight (pounds)	Calories burned in 1.5 hours
Christina	92	533
Miguel	84	486
Sara	108	625
Xavier	117	677

Then calculate the number of bananas to buy for each person. Divide calories burned by the calories in one banana.

Christina: 533 calories burned ÷ 125 calories per banana = 4.2 bananas

Miguel: 486 calories burned ÷ 125 calories per banana = 3.8 bananas

Sara: 625 calories burned ÷ 125 calories per banana = 5 bananas

Xavier: 677 calories burned ÷ 125 calories per banana = 5.4 bananas

Round up the answers to the nearest whole banana. The friends will need 20 bananas to equal the amount of calories they burn. But they probably won't eat them all at once!

CON "CLUE" SION

Here is one last mystery. What do the clues describe?

1)   It sees into the future and foresees storms.

2)   It serves pi you cannot eat.

3)   It catches the flu, but does not get sick.

4)   It tells volumes about space.

5)   It finds the best discount at all costs.

6)   It tells time, but does not wear a watch.

THE CLUES DESCRIBE MATH, your powerful, take-anywhere, mystery-solving tool.

GLOSSARY

area (AIR-ee-uh)—the amount of surface in a given boundary

average (AV-uh-rij)—a measure of the middle of a group of numbers; average is found by adding all the numbers in a group together then dividing the sum by the total of numbers in the group

calorie (KA-luh-ree)—a measurement of the amount of energy that food gives you

denominator (di-NOM-uh-nay-tur)—the number below the line in a fraction; it shows how many equal parts the whole number can be divided into

diameter (dye-AM-uh-tur)—the length of a line segment that runs from one side to another in a circle through the center

dosage (DOH-sihj)—an amount of something, such as a medicine

numerator (NOO-muh-ray-tur)—the number above the line in a fraction; it shows how many parts of the denominator are taken

time zone (TIME ZOHN)— a region in which the same time is used

tsunami (tsoo-NAH-mee)—a large, destructive wave caused by an underwater earthquake

volume (VOL-yuhm)—the amount of space taken up by an object

READ MORE

Stille, Darlene R. *The Case of the Soda Explosion and Other True Science Mysteries for You to Solve.* Seriously True Mysteries. Mankato, Minn.: Capstone Press, 2012.

Stosch, Dawn. *Science Math.* Math Alive. New York: Marshall Cavendish Benchmark, 2009.

Wingard-Nelson, Rebecca. *Problem Solving and Word Problem Smarts!* Math Smarts! Berkeley Heights, N.J.: Enslow Publishers, 2012.

Yoder, Eric, and Natalie Yoder. *65 Short Stories You Solve with Math!* One Minute Mysteries. Washington D.C.: Science, Naturally! 2010.

INTERNET SITES

FactHound offers a safe, fun way to find Internet sites related to this book. All of the sites on FactHound have been researched by our staff.

Here's all you do:

Visit *www.facthound.com*

Type in this code: 9781429676243

Check out projects, games and lots more at
www.capstonekids.com

INDEX